How We Use Plants

for Medicine and Health

Sally Morgan

WAYLAND

First published in 2007 by Wayland

Copyright © Wayland 2007

Wayland
338 Euston Road
London NW1 3BH

Wayland Australia
Level 17/207 Kent Street
Sydney, NSW 2000

Editor: Camilla Lloyd
Designer: Matthew Lilly
Picture Researcher: Sally Morgan

Picture Acknowledgments: The author and publisher would
like to thank the following for allowing these pictures to be
reproduced in this publication. Cover: Ecoscene,
Mediscan/Alamy tr, Alan Oliver/Alamy cr; Ecoscene: 4, 5, 6,
8, 9, 10, 11, 12, 13, 15, 16, 18, 19, 20, 21, 22, 23, 24, 26,
27, 28; B.Lawton/Corbis: 7; Alan Oliver/Alamy: 14,
Mediscan/Alamy: 1, 17, Edward Parker/Alamy: 25, Nigel
Cattlin/Alamy: 26 bl.
With special thanks to Ecoscene.

British Library Cataloguing in Publication Data:
Morgan, Sally
How we use plants for medicine
1. Medicinal plants - Juvenile literature 2. Herbs -
Therapeutic use - Juvenile literature
I. Title
581.6'34

ISBN: 978 07502 5065 8

Printed in China

Wayland is a division of Hachette Children's Books

Contents

Plants for medicine and health

Plants are not just used for food. They are important for our health too. Plants have been used to make **medicines** for thousands of years. They are used in **cosmetics** and skin care products, too.

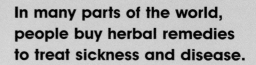

In many parts of the world, people buy herbal remedies to treat sickness and disease.

Herbal medicine involves the use of plants as **remedies** to treat injuries and disease. Remedies can come from any part of a plant including flowers, **stems**, **leaves**, fruits, roots or the bark. Recently people have started to take a greater interest in these **traditional** remedies.

The foxglove can be used to make medicine to treat heart disease.

Today, about one quarter of all modern medicines, such as pills, are either made from plants or based on plant products. About 50,000 different types of plants are used to make medicines and herbal remedies. Some people prefer to use natural medicines. For many of the world's poorest people, plant remedies are important because people can find and collect the plants themselves.

5

Making herbal remedies

Plants that contain useful medicines have to be **harvested** and the useful part taken out. Most plants are picked from the wild. Some plants are grown as **crops**.

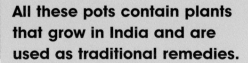

All these pots contain plants that grow in India and are used as traditional remedies.

Plant remedies are prepared in a number of different ways. An **infusion** is made in the same way as a cup of tea. Hot water is poured over plant leaves, left for a few minutes and then the water is drunk. Tougher materials such as bark and root are boiled in water for about 20 minutes. A **tincture** is prepared by grinding the plant material into a powder, which is then mixed with alcohol and water.

This cup contains an infusion of sage and thyme.

As herbal remedies become more popular, more plants are collected from the wild. Sadly, this is threatening the survival of some of the rarer plants.

Antiseptics and disinfectants

Bacteria are **microorganisms** that are far too small to be seen with the eye. They are found everywhere – in the air, on surfaces, on the ground and even in water. Most bacteria are harmless, but some can cause disease.

Neem trees grow in India where they are used to make soap and shampoo. The tree can also be used to help with digestion and diabetes.

Australian Aborigines use leaves from the tea tree to treat cuts. They crush the leaves and place them on the skin.

Disinfectants are used to kill bacteria, especially in the kitchen and bathroom.

Antiseptics are put on the skin and wounds to kill harmful bacteria. There are many plants that we use to make products that kill bacteria, including coconut, garlic, the neem tree and the tea tree. Tea tree oil is a powerful natural antiseptic that is several times stronger than a household disinfectant.

Did You Know?
During the 1770s, Captain James Cook and his crew named the tree "tea tree," because they used the leaves for making tea.

Keeping clean

It is important to wash your skin and hair and to brush your teeth. This helps the body to stay healthy. Body **odour** is produced by sweat. It can be avoided by washing the skin with soap every day and using **deodorants** to disguise the smell of sweat.

The oil from coconuts is used in soaps, shampoos and hand creams.

Have A Go!

- Simple, homemade shampoos can be just as good as some bought in the shops. Make your own shampoo by putting the following in a blender: 1 tablespoon olive oil, 1 egg (remove the shell), 1 tablespoon lemon juice, and 1 teaspoon apple cider vinegar. Use immediately.

Soaps can be made with oils that come from plants such as jojoba, tea tree, almond, grape seed and coconut. Shampoo is used to remove oil, sweat and dirt from hair. Shampoo contains a mixture of ingredients, many of which are plant oils and herbs.

Lavender grows wild in meadows. The oil from the flower has a great smell. A few drops can be added to warm water to make a relaxing bath.

Healthy teeth

Every time you eat, food is left on your teeth. The food is eaten by bacteria. Bacteria and the leftover food form a sticky layer over your teeth called **plaque**. When you eat sugary foods the bacteria produce acids. The acids attack **enamel** on the outside of teeth. Eventually a hole appears in the enamel and the tooth starts to decay.

The Apaches, a native American tribe, use fibres from the leaves of the yucca plant to make dental floss.

It's A Question!

Why is flossing important?

Plaque must be removed every day by brushing your teeth with toothpaste. Many plant extracts are used in toothpaste, the most popular being mint. Others include chamomile, myrrh, sage, eucalyptus and tea tree. People in South Asia use the white milky liquid from the trunk and branches of the banyan tree to ease toothache.

Mint is used in toothpaste to give a fresh taste that leaves the teeth feeling really clean.

Skin care

Suncreams are rubbed on to the skin to stop it burning in the sun.

There are many types of skin creams and soaps. For example, there are creams to prevent the skin from drying, to treat acne (spots), and to prevent sunburn. Acne is caused by the skin producing too much oil. Bacteria feed on the oil and this causes spots to form.

Cleaning the skin helps to prevent acne. Plant antiseptics, such as sandalwood and tea tree oil are used in skin cleansers to stop bacteria growing on the skin.

Have A Go!

- Tea tree oil can be used to treat acne. Clean the face with soap. Then partly fill the sink with warm water and add a few drops of tea tree oil. Use this to rinse the face.

In the past, plants such as the soapwort were used to make soap because they contained substances called saponins. Saponins form a **lather** in water that cleans the skin.

The roots of the pink ragged robin contain saponins, which can be used to wash clothes.

15

Painkillers

People take **painkillers** to stop the feeling of pain in the body. One of the most common uses of painkillers is to stop headaches. Painkillers are also used when the body has been injured and there is pain from the bruising and swelling.

The unripe seeds of the opium poppy contain a milky juice which is collected, dried and used to make morphine.

Did You Know?
Aspirin has been used for thousands of years. The ancient Greeks used willow bark to treat a fever.

Many painkillers are based on parts of plants. The most common painkiller is aspirin. Originally, aspirin was obtained from the white willow tree. Nowadays, aspirin is made **artificially**. Another important painkiller is morphine, which comes from the opium poppy. This is a very strong painkiller and has to be recommended by doctors.

Tablets containing painkillers are swallowed. They dissolve in the stomach and go into the blood.

Taking too many painkillers can harm the body and even kill you. Some people become **addicted** to painkillers. They cannot stop taking them and they have to be treated for their addiction by doctors.

Fighting disease

It is important for our bodies to be as strong as they can be to be able to fight off the germs that can cause disease. Parts of some plants can help prevent illnesses and protect against disease.

A hot drink made of elderberries can help protect against germs.

The echinacea plant is believed to help protect against colds and the 'flu.

Every year, more than one million people die from the disease, malaria. One of the best treatments for malaria is quinine and this comes from the bark of the cinchona tree. Another traditional treatment is neem tree oil mixed with coriander and ginger.

Neem tree oil comes from the fruits and seeds of the tree. It can be rubbed into wounds to stop infection.

Melia azedirachta
planted on - 27-7-93

Treating disease

Garlic is used to treat heart disease and asthma. Ginger can be used to treat arthritis and it can also stop travel sickness and help digestion.

Garlic is grown as a crop. It has been used for thousands of years as a remedy.

Coconut can be used for digestive problems, such as diarrhoea and to treat heart disease. Juice from the cranberry fruit is used to treat urinary infections. The insides of seed pods from the tamarind (a type of tree) can be smeared on painful joints, used for sore throats or to treat people with sunstroke.

Hawthorn is a hedgerow plant that flowers in May. The fruits from the plant can be used to treat heart disease.

Fighting and treating cancer

Cancer is a disease that kills millions of people each year. Many cancer treatments use plant products. The rosy periwinkle plant is found in the rainforest. It contains a product that can be used to treat leukaemia (a cancer of the blood and the bone marrow).

Did You Know?

The clippings from yew hedges can be collected and used to make a drug to fight breast cancer. Each year, gardeners in Britain gather about 200 tonnes a year of yew clippings.

The rosy periwinkle has pink flowers and it grows in the rainforests of Madagascar in the Indian Ocean.

Leaves of the evening primrose can be used to make an infusion to help people to sleep. The whole plant is used to make a painkiller.

Amazingly about two thirds of the cancer drugs in use today come from plants. For example, a substance from the yew tree and an oil from the evening primrose plant are used to treat breast cancer. A substance in brown rice helps stomach cancer. A number of rainforest plants contain substances that are used to treat cancer.

Every part of the yew is poisonous to eat except the red flesh around the seed. However, part of the plant can protect against cancer.

23

Discovering new plants

Only about one in every five types of plant have ever been studied for their medical uses. This means that there are many more plants that may contain parts that could be used to cure a disease in the future.

These people are identifying the different plants found in a rainforest in Indonesia.

Medical companies send people to rainforests and other remote places in the world to search for new plants. The plants are then tested in a laboratory to see if they contain things that could be used in medicines. If they do, the plants are tested further. This testing takes a long time and it may be many years between finding a new plant and making a new medicine.

These racks are stacked with medicinal plants that have been harvested in Brazil.

Some of the world's plants are under threat because their **habitat** is being destroyed, for example, the rainforests. It is important that the world's plants are protected as they could help to cure diseases in the future.

How the aloe vera plant is used

Aloe vera is a cactus-like plant that has thick, fleshy leaves. It grows in desert habitats and other dry places. Inside the leaves is a jelly-like substance that has many uses.

Cosmetics:
Dried aloe vera is used in cosmetics and skin care creams.

Drink:
Aloe vera juice is made into a healthy and popular drink.

Treatment for the skin:
Gel from inside the leaves can be smeared over sunburn, wounds, bruises, insect stings and acne (spots).

Digestive aid:
Aloe vera gel can be made into a juice. Drinking the juice can help digestion.

Make your own herbal salve!

Marigolds (also called Calendula) are very easy plants to grow. The leaves contain a mild antiseptic and can be used to treat minor rashes, burns, cuts and athlete's foot.

Step 1

Buy a packet of marigold seeds and in early summer plant the seeds into garden soil or in a window box. The first flowers appear within about six weeks. You can collect some marigold leaves to make a herbal **salve** to rub over a rash, burn or cut. You will need about three handfuls of marigold leaves, some cold pressed extra virgin olive oil, wheatgerm oil, a clean glass jar and lid, a bowl, a measuring jug, a piece of waxed paper, muslin, and a small, dark bottle. Make sure that you wear a long-sleeved top and some rubber gloves to make your salve.

Step 2

Rinse your leaves in water and leave them to dry. Place your leaves in a small bowl or a mortar and add a few teaspoons of cold pressed extra virgin olive oil. Use a wooden spoon or pestle to grind them up, adding a little more olive oil if needed.

Step 3

Place the ground up leaves in a clean jar and add some more olive oil. There needs to be about 4 cm of oil above the leaves. Cover the jar with a piece of waxed paper and then screw the lid in place. Stick a label on the jar, listing the contents and the date. Leave on a sunny window ledge for one month, gently swirling the mix each day.

Step 4

Then remove the lid and paper and tie a piece of clean muslin over the top of the jar. Strain the oil through the muslin into a measuring jug. Make a marking on the side of the jug to show how much liquid is present. Now add one part wheatgerm oil to nine parts of the olive oil and marigold mixture. Mix well.

Step 5

Pour this into a dark bottle. It will keep for several months. This is your salve. Make sure you label the bottle with a list of the contents and the date and the words 'For external use only'. Now you can use your salve to sooth skin that has been grazed or has a small cut. It can be kept for up to a year.

Glossary

addicted when the body or mind is dependent on something.

antiseptic substance that kills or slows down the growth of harmful bacteria.

artificial not natural, made by people.

bacteria tiny organism that cannot be seen with the eye, some bacteria cause disease.

cosmetics make-up for the face.

crops a group of plants grown by people for a special use.

deodorant a spray or cream to mask body smells.

disinfectant something that destroys bacteria.

enamel a layer that covers and protects teeth.

habitat the natural home of a plant or animal.

harvested gathered, collected.

herbal relating to the use of herbs.

infusion a drink made by soaking something in a liquid.

lather froth produced by soap or shampoo.

leaf (pl leaves) part of a plant, a blade that is attached to the stem.

medicine a substance used to treat sickness and disease.

microorganisms tiny organisms such as bacteria that can only be seen under a microscope.

odour smell.

painkiller a substance that stops the feeling of pain in the body.

plaque a sticky layer on teeth that is formed from the bacteria in food.

remedy a treatment for a disease.

salve a soothing, healing balm or gel.

stem part of a plant that supports the leaves.

tincture a solution made from plants, alcohol and water.

traditional a way of doing something that has been used for a long time.

Further information

Books

Looking at Plants, Flowers, Fruits and Seeds by Sally Morgan, Belitha Press, 2002

How does your Garden Grow? Great Gardening for green-fingered kids by Clare Matthews and Clive Nichols, Hamlyn Gardening, 2005

Young Gardener by Stefan T. & Beverley Buczacki and Anthea Sieveking, Francis Lincoln, 2006

Kids Herb Book for Children of All Ages, by Lesley Tierr, Robert D. Reed Publishers, 2006

Why Should I Wash? And other questions about Keeping Clean and Healthy by Angela Royston, Heinemann Library, 2004

Personal Hygiene (Keeping Healthy) by Carol Ballard, Wayland, 2007

Answers

P12 flossing removes plaque from between teeth and helps to stop gum disease

Index